Java Programming For Beginners

The Evolution Of Java And Some Basics

Salem M. Kennedy

Table of Content

The History and Evolution of Java

About Java and History :

1. Java was planned by Sun Microsystems in the mid 1990s.

2. Basic point of java was to take care of the issue of interfacing numerous family machines together.

3. Project was fruitless on the grounds that nobody needed to utilize it.

4. Earlier Name of Java : **OAK**

5. Creator of Java : **James Gosling** (the father of Java)

6. As there was another language called Oak , they decided to rename OAK. New name was given to OAK , OAK was renamed Java in **1994**

7. Java was publicly released on : **May 27, 1995**

8. Java was targeted at : **Internet development**

9. Applets Had early support from c

Language was created with 5 main goals:

1. It should be object oriented

2. A single representation of a program could be executed on multiple operating systems

3. It should fully support network programming

4. It should execute code from remote sources securely

5. It should be easy to use

What is Java?

Java is widely used programming language which has wide verity of applications such as desktop applications, Mobile Applications, Enterprise applications etc.
[box]
Java is a –

1. Class Based and Object Oriended Programming Language

2. Computing platform

3. Fast, Secure, and Reliable.

4. Free

5. General Purpose

6. Concurrent

Four primary goals in the creation of the Java language :

1. It should be "simple, object-oriented and familiar".

2. It should be "robust and secure".

3. It should be "architecture-neutral and portable".

4. It should execute with "high performance".

Some of the Versions of Java :

Java Version	Release Date	Year
JDK 1.0	January 21	1996
JDK 1.1	February 19	1997
J2SE 1.2	December 8	1998
J2SE 1.3	May 8	2000
J2SE 1.4	February 6	2002
J2SE 5.0	September 30	2004
Java SE 6	December 11	2006
Java SE 7	July 28	2011

How Java Related to C# ?

1.   After the production of Java, Microsoft built up the C# language and C# is firmly identified with Java.

2.   Many of C#'s highlights legitimately parallel Java. Both Java and C# share a similar general C++-style sentence structure, bolster conveyed programming, and use a similar article model.

3.   Though there are a few contrasts among Java and C#, yet the general feel of these dialects is fundamentally the same as.

4.   If you definitely know C#, at that point learning Java will be simple and the other way around

5.   Java and C# are advanced for two distinct kinds of registering situations.

6.   C# and Java Both Languages are drew from C++.

7.   Both Languages are equipped for making cross stage versatile   program   code.

Consider Scenario of Java Programming Language

1.   Java is made by Sun Micro System.

2.   Java Compiler produces Intermediate code called Byte Code.

3.   Byte Code i.e moderate code is executed by the Run Time Environment.

4.   In Java Run Time Environment is called as "JVM" [Java Virtual Machine]

5.   If we have JVM as of now introduced on any stage then JVM can deliver machine subordinate Code dependent on the middle of the road code.

Java Vs C Sharp

Here are some differences between Java and C Sharp.

Point	Java	C#
Development	Sun Microsystem	Microsoft
Development Year	1995	2000
Data Types	Less Primitive DT	More Primitive DT
Struct Concept	Not Supported	Supported
Switch Case	String in Switch Not Allowed	String in Switch Allowed
Delegates	Absent	Supported

Re-commanded Reading :

External Article	Link
Difference between Java and C#	CodeProject
Similarities Between C# and Java	MSDN

Java's Contribution to the Internet (World Wide Web):

1.   Great component of the java is that java is stage free.

2.   It can word on any network,any working framework in this way making projects progressively adaptable.

3.   In expansion to improving web programming when all is said in done, Java advanced another kind of organized program considered the applet that changed the way the online world idea about substance.

4.   Portability and Security of java makes World wide web to spread crosswise over globe.

A. Java Applets :

1. An applet is a unique sort of Java program that is intended to be transmitted over the Internet and naturally executed by a Java-good internet browser.

2. Applet can be downloaded on request.

3. Applet projects can be run on insect java good program.Applets are intended to be small programs.

4. They are typically used to display data provided by the server, handle user input, or provide simple functions, such as a loan calculator, that execute locally, rather than on the server.

5. In essence, the applet allows some **functionality to be moved from the server to the client**.

B. Security :

1. Applets can be downloaded to **client PC .**

2. They are executed autonomously without getting to different pieces of client's PC.

3. The capacity of Java gives security and in this way Java substantiate itself increasingly secure.

C. Portability :

1. Java Programming is Portable.

2. . Java Program is Operating System Independent..

3. Java Program is converted into **byte code and byte code is executed by JVM**. [See how Java Code is Portable ?]

4. Java Applets are thus portable and can be downloaded from any place in globe and can be executed on java compatible browser thus making java programs portable.

How java is Considered as Platform Independent and Portable ?

In this tutorial we have covered step by step discussion about –

1. Which features makes java Platform Independent ?

2. Why Java is Platform Independent ?

3. Why Java is considered as Secure and Portable Language ?

A. Java is considered as Portable because –

Java is Considered as Platform independent because of many different reasons which are listed below –

1. Output of a Java compiler is **Non Executable Code i.e Bytecode**.

2. Bytecode is a **highly optimized set of instructions**

3. Bytecode is executed by Java run-time system, which is called the Java Virtual Machine (**JVM**).

Important Note :

As the output of Java Compiler is Non Executable Code we can consider it as Secure (it cannot be used for automated execution of malicious programs).

4. JVM is an **interpreter**.

5. JVM accepts **Bytecode as input and execute it**.

6. Translating a Java program into bytecode makes it much easier to run a program in a wide variety of environments because only **the JVM needs to be implemented for each platform**.

7. For a given System we have Run-time package , once **JVM is installed for particular system** then any java program can run on it.

8. However Internal details of **JVM will differ from platform to platform** but still all understand the **Same Java Bytecode**.

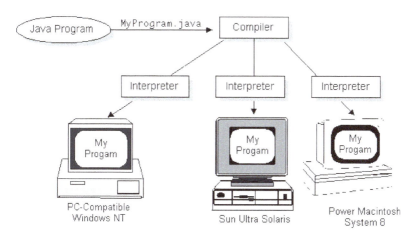

How Java Program is Platform Independent ?

B. Why Java Code is Safe ?

1. Java program is **executed by the JVM**.

2. The JVM **prevent** java code from **generating side effects outside** of the system.

3. Safety is also enhanced by certain restrictions that exist in the Java language.

C. Interpreter are slower than Compiler

Java Code is Executed by JVM (interpreter).Other programming language uses compiler which can create executable code much faster then why we are using Interpreter.

1. When a program is interpreted, it generally runs slower than the same program would run if compiled to executable code.

2. In Java Compiler will generate **ByteCode which is highly optimized**.

3. Thus running highly optimized code using interpreter makes execution of **java program faster**.

11 Features of Java Programming Language

Simple :

- Java is Easy to write and more readable and eye catching.

- Java has a concise, cohesive set of features that makes it easy to learn and use.

- Most of the concepts are drew from C++ thus making Java learning simpler.

Secure :

- Java program cannot harm other system thus making it secure.

- Java provides a secure means of creating Internet applications.

- Java provides secure way to access web applications.

Portable :

- Java programs can execute in any environment for which there is a Java run-time system.(JVM)

- Java programs can be run on any platform (Linux,Window,Mac)

- Java programs can be transferred over world wide web (e.g applets)

Object-oriented :

- Java programming is object-oriented programming language.

- Like C++ java provides most of the object oriented features.

- Java is pure OOP. Language. (while C++ is semi object oriented)

Robust :

- Java encourages error-free programming by being strictly typed and performing run-time checks.

Multithreaded :

- Java provides integrated support for multithreaded programming.

Architecture-neutral :

- Java is not tied to a specific machine or operating system architecture.

- Machine Independent i.e Java is independent of hardware .

Interpreted :

- Java supports cross-platform code through the use of Java bytecode.

- Bytecode can be interpreted on any platform by JVM.

High performance :

- Bytecodes are highly optimized.

- JVM can executed them much faster .

Distributed :

- Java was designed with the distributed environment.

- Java can be transmit,run over internet.

Dynamic :

- Java programs carry with them substantial amounts of run-time type information that is used to verify and resolve accesses to objects at run time.

Tools Required for Java

Steps to Download Latest Version of Java :

1. Navigate to Link : Download JDK

2. Click on the Download Java [Java Platform (JDK) 7u17]

3. After Clicking on the Java Logo it will redirect you to the actual download page.

4. On the download page you have to click on radio button to accept terms and conditions of oracle.

Java SE Development Kit 7u25

You must accept the Oracle Binary Code License Agreement for Java SE to download this software.

Thank you for accepting the Oracle Binary Code License Agreement for Java SE; you may now download this software.

Product / File Description	File Size	Download
Linux x86	80.38 MB	⬇ jdk-7u25-linux-i586.rpm
Linux x86	93.12 MB	⬇ jdk-7u25-linux-i586.tar.gz
Linux x64	81.46 MB	⬇ jdk-7u25-linux-x64.rpm
Linux x64	91.85 MB	⬇ jdk-7u25-linux-x64.tar.gz
Mac OS X x64	144.43 MB	⬇ jdk-7u25-macosx-x64.dmg
Solaris x86 (SVR4 package)	136.02 MB	⬇ jdk-7u25-solaris-i586.tar.Z
Solaris x86	92.22 MB	⬇ jdk-7u25-solaris-i586.tar.gz
Solaris x64 (SVR4 package)	22.77 MB	⬇ jdk-7u25-solaris-x64.tar.Z
Solaris x64	15.09 MB	⬇ jdk-7u25-solaris-x64.tar.gz
Solaris SPARC (SVR4 package)	136.16 MB	⬇ jdk-7u25-solaris-sparc.tar.Z
Solaris SPARC	95.5 MB	⬇ jdk-7u25-solaris-sparc.tar.gz
Solaris SPARC 64-bit (SVR4 package)	23.05 MB	⬇ jdk-7u25-solaris-sparcv9.tar.Z
Solaris SPARC 64-bit	17.67 MB	⬇ jdk-7u25-solaris-sparcv9.tar.gz
Windows x86	89.09 MB	⬇ jdk-7u25-windows-i586.exe
Windows x64	90.66 MB	⬇ jdk-7u25-windows-x64.exe

5. Select appropriate version as per requirement.

6. Click on download link after that downloading will be started . Setup is nearly about 75-80 mb.

[box]I am running java on Window 7 (64-bit) therefor i will select suitable version for me – **[jdk-7u17-windows-x64.exe]**

Most Popular Java Editors :

While surfing web i come across this site . This site provides detailed explanation of all the popular editors for creating java applications. [Here] List of Some Useful Java Editors are :

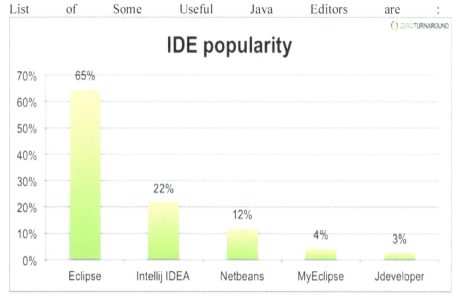

Editor	Cost	License
Eclipse 3.0	Free	Open Source (CPL)
Netbeans 3.x	Free	Sun Micro System
JBuilder X (Borland)	$499	Borland
IntelliJ IDEA	$499	IntelliJ IDEA
JDeveloper	$219	Oracle

5 Most Popular Free Java Editors for Beginners !!

1. Eclipse IDE

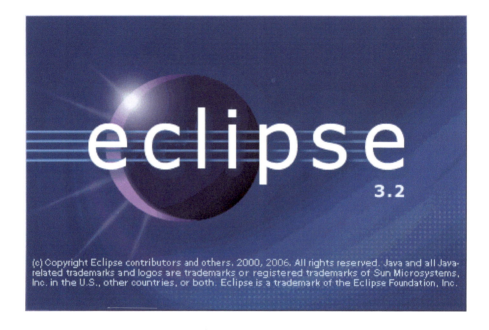

2. Netbeans

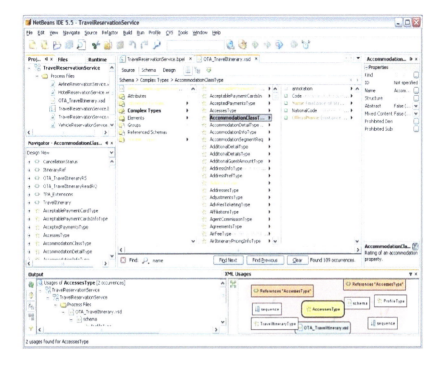

3. Notepad++

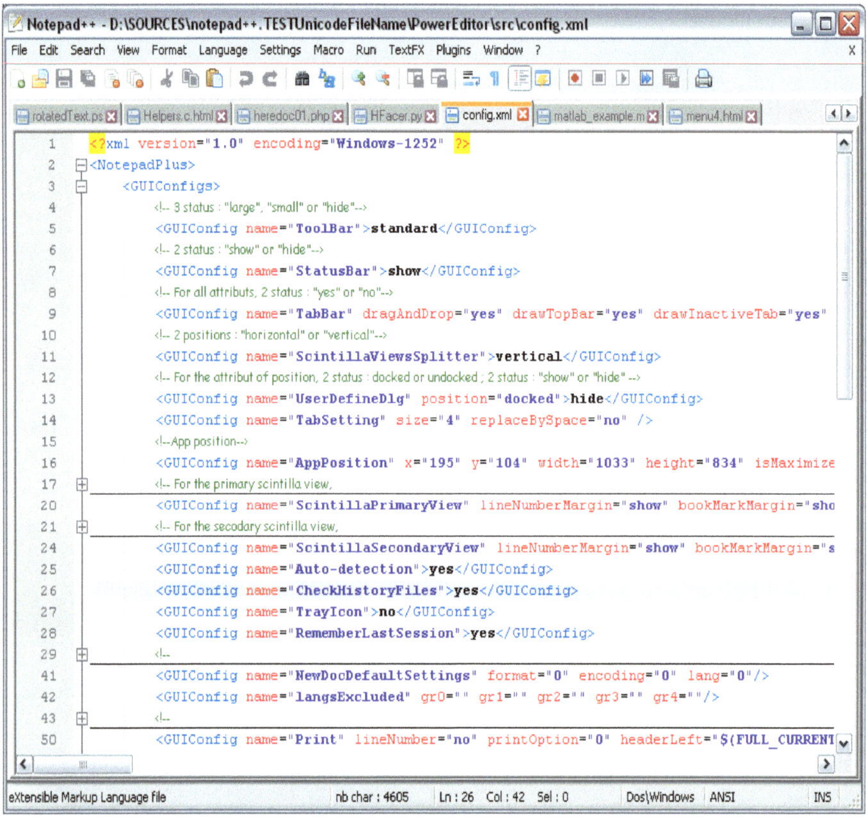
Notepad++ - D:\SOURCES\notepad++.TESTUnicodeFileName\PowerEditor\src\config.xml
File Edit Search View Format Language Settings Macro Run TextFX Plugins Window ?
rotatedText.ps
Helpers.c.html
heredoc01.php
HFacer.py
config.xml
matlab_example.m
menu4.html
<?xml version="1.0" encoding="Windows-1252" ?>
<NotepadPlus>
<GUIConfigs>
<!-- 3 status : "large", "small" or "hide"-->
<GUIConfig name="ToolBar">standard</GUIConfig>
<!-- 2 status : "show" or "hide"-->
<GUIConfig name="StatusBar">show</GUIConfig>
<!-- For all attributs, 2 status : "yes" or "no"-->
<GUIConfig name="TabBar" dragAndDrop="yes" drawTopBar="yes" drawInactiveTab="yes"
<!-- 2 positions : "horizontal" or "vertical"-->
<GUIConfig name="ScintillaViewsSplitter">vertical</GUIConfig>
<!-- For the attribut of position, 2 status : docked or undocked ; 2 status : "show" or "hide" -->
<GUIConfig name="UserDefineDlg" position="docked">hide</GUIConfig>
<GUIConfig name="TabSetting" size="4" replaceBySpace="no" />
<!--App position-->
<GUIConfig name="AppPosition" x="195" y="104" width="1033" height="834" isMaximize
<!-- For the primary scintilla view,
<GUIConfig name="ScintillaPrimaryView" lineNumberMargin="show" bookMarkMargin="sho
<!-- For the secodary scintilla view,
<GUIConfig name="ScintillaSecondaryView" lineNumberMargin="show" bookMarkMargin="s
<GUIConfig name="Auto-detection">yes</GUIConfig>
<GUIConfig name="CheckHistoryFiles">yes</GUIConfig>
<GUIConfig name="TrayIcon">no</GUIConfig>
<GUIConfig name="RememberLastSession">yes</GUIConfig>
<!--
<GUIConfig name="NewDocDefaultSettings" format="0" encoding="0" lang="0"/>
<GUIConfig name="langsExcluded" gr0="" gr1="" gr2="" gr3="" gr4=""/>
<!--
<GUIConfig name="Print" lineNumber="no" printOption="0" headerLeft="$(FULL_CURRENT
eXtensible Markup Language file
nb char : 4605
Ln : 26 Col : 42 Sel : 0
Dos\Windows
ANSI
INS

4. Editplus

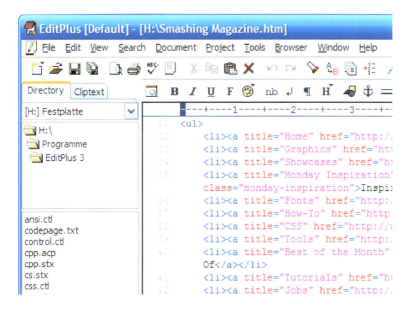

5. Jcreator

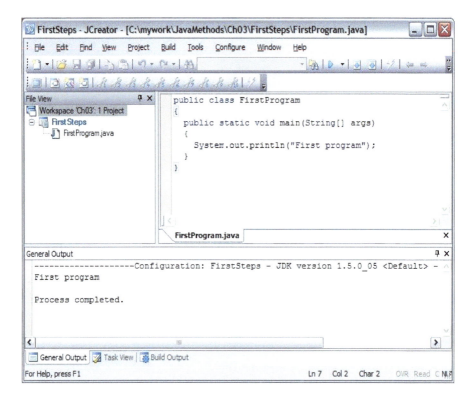

Data Types, Variables & Operators in Java

Variables in Java Programming

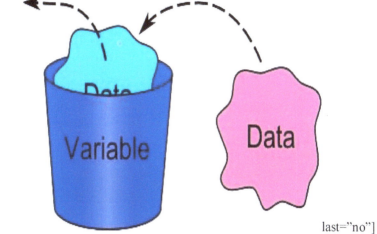

[one_half   last="no"]
[/one_half]Variables in Java Programming is something that can be changed, such as a characteristic or value. If we consider programming concept then we can say that variable is something which can store a value. It is container for storing a value. Variable name may be given by programmer.

Some Rules of Variable Naming Convention :

1. Variable names are **case-sensitive**.

2. A variable's name **can be any legal identifier**.

3. It can contain Unicode **letter,Digits and Two Special Characters** such as Underscore and dollar Sign.

4. Length of Variable name can be any number.

5. Its necessary to use Alphabet at the start (however we can use underscore , but do not use it)

6. Some auto generated variables may contain '$' sign. But try to avoid using Dollar Sign.

7. **White space** is not permitted.

8. **Special Characters** are not allowed.

9. **Digit at start** is not allowed.

10. Subsequent characters may be **letters, digits, dollar signs, or underscore characters**.

11. Variable name must not be a **keyword or reserved word**.

[468×60]

Some Standard Conventions Used :

1. Never Use Dollar Or Underscore as First Letter

- Dollar Sign and Underscore as First Character in Variable name is allowed but still its not good programming Style to use it as First Character.

- Generally we use Underscore in "Constant Value" variable.

```
static final int TOTAL_NUM = 10;
```

```java
static final int MAX_COUNT = 20;
```

*Final is nothing but constant value in Java (In c we use const)

2. Capitalization of First Character of Second Word

- If variable name contain two words then write first letter of second word in Capital Case.

- If variable name contain single word then write that word in small case.

[468×60]

Example : Multiple Words in Variable Name

```
sumOfNumber
```

```
firstNumber
```

```
skinColor
```

Example : Single Word in Variable Name

```
sum
```

```
first
```

```
last
```

The Java programming language defines the following kinds of variables:

1. Instance Variables

2. Static Variables

3. Local Variables

Instance Variables (Non-Static Fields)

1. Non-Static Variables are called as **Instance Variable**.

2. Instance variables are variables **within a class but outside any method**.

3. Whenever we create an object of class then **we can have certain attributes of the class that are unique for each object** , that attribute variable is called as "**Instance Variable**".

4. Individual states of objects is stored in "non-static fields". (instance variable).

5. **Non-static fields are also known as instance variables** because their values are unique to each instance of a class (to each object, in other words).

Sample Example

```
Class Person
{
String name;
```

```
int     age;
String gender;
};


Person P1,P2,P3;
```

In the above example we have created class "Person". We can have different Attributes of Class Person such as name,age,gender . These attributes are unique for different objects. Such as for object P1's name can be different from P2's name. Such variables that are unique for individual object is called Instance Variable.

Class Variables (Static Fields)

1. A class variable is any field **declared with the static modifier**.

2. Exactly one copy of static or class variable is created , regardless of how many times the class has been instantiated.

3. Suppose we have created 5 objects then all of the objects can share same variable.

   Example :

```
Class Person
{
String name;
int     age;
String gender;

static String city = "Pune";
```

```
};

Person P1,P2,P3;
```

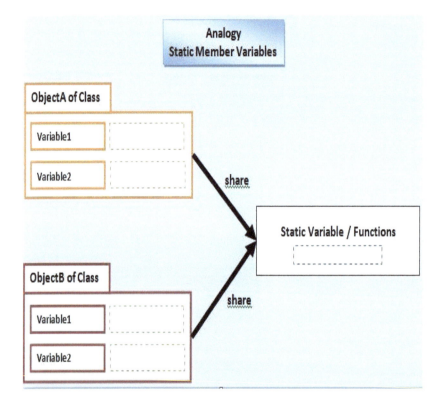

Local Variables

1. In order to store Temporary state we use local variables.

2. Generally local variables are declared in

   the **methods,constructors,blocks**.

3. "count" is local variable in following code snippet.

4. Destroyed when method gets executed completely.

Example :

```
int counting(int n1,int n2)
  {
  int count;
  count = n1 + n2;
  return(count);
  }
```

Primitive Data Types in Java Programming Language :

Data type is nothing but the type of the data. Each Variable in Java must have certain type associated with it which tells us what kind of data a variable can store.

Data Types in Java Programming Language are classified into two main groups – Primitive and Reference Data Types.

A primitive Data Types are :

1. Data types are predefined by the Java language.

2. Predefined data types are Reserved keyword so we cannot use them as variable name inside program/application

3. Primitive values do not share state with other primitive values.

4. Total Number of Primitive Data Types in Java Programming is 8

5. All Primitive Data Types have respective Wrapper Classes i.e **Integer** is wrapper class for primitive type **int**

Primitive Data Types are –

Primitive Data Types in Java :			
Boolean	char	byte	int
Short	long	float	double

Classification of Data Types in Java Programming Language

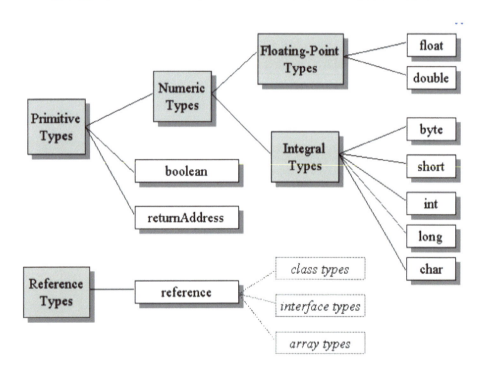

Data Type and Other Details

byte	Signed Integer	0	8 bits
short	Signed Integer	0	16 bits
int	Signed Integer	0	32 bits
long	Signed Integer	0	64 bits
float	Floating Number	0.0	32 bit
double	Floating Number	0.0	64 bit

Integer Data Type :

1. Integer Data Type is used to store integer value.

2. Integer Data Type is Primitive Data Type in Java Programming Language.

3. Integer Data Type have respective Wrapper Class – "**Integer**".

4. Integer Data Type is able to store both unsigned ans signed integer values so Java opted signed,unsigned concept of C/C++.

Integer Data Type Can have 4 types of Values these are listed below table –

Name	Width	Range
long	64	−9,223,372,036,854,775,808 to 9,223,372,036,854,775,807

Name	Width	Range
int	32	–2,147,483,648 to 2,147,483,647
short	16	–32,768 to 32,767
byte	8	–128 to 127

Live Example : Declaring Integer Variable in Java Programming

```java
Class IntDemo
{
public static void main(String args[])
  {
  int number=0;
  System.out.println("Total Number : " + number);
  }
```

Float Data Type :

1. Floating Data Type is used to store float value.

2. Floating Data Type is Primitive Data Type in Java Programming Language.

3. Floating Data Type have respective Wrapper Class – "**Float or Double**".

float Data Type Can store 2 types of Values these are listed below –

1. Float

2. Double

[468×60]

float	Variables of this type can have values from -3.4E38 (-3.4 * 1038) to +3.4E38 (+3.4 * 1038) and occupy 4 bytes in memory. Values are represented with approximately 7 decimal digits accuracy
double	Variables of this type can have values from -1.7E308 (-1.7 * 10308) to +1.7E308 (+1.7 * 10308) and occupy 8 bytes in memory. Values are represented with approximately 17 decimal digits accuracy. The smallest non-zero value that you can have is roughly (4.9 * 10–324).

Live Example : Declaring Integer Variable in Java Programming

```
Class FloatDemo
{
public static void main(String args[])
```

```
{
float fval = 10.0f;
System.out.println("Total Number : " + fval);
}
}
```

Float Type : Some Notes

1. In Java any value declared with decimal point is by default of type **double**.

2. Suppose we have to assign float value then we must use 'f' or 'F' literal to specify that current value is "Float".

3. Specify "E" or "e" for values which contain exponent.

Way 1 : How to Declare Double Variable

```
Class FloatDemo
{
public static void main(String args[])
  {
  double d1 = 10;
  System.out.println("Total Number : " + fval);
  }
}
```

- We have assigned integer value to the Double . (i.e we are assigning lower value of inside bigger variable , no need to typecast)

- double keyword is used to declare double variable.

Way 2 : How to Declare float Variable

```java
float fval = 10.4F;
```

Way 3 : Using Exponent In Double Value

```java
float electronMass = 9E-28F;
```

another example

```java
double lightSpeed = 3.8E8;
```

Way 4 : Declaring Fix Value

```java
final int meter_in_cm = 100;
```

Character data Type : Java Primitive Data Types

1. In Java, the data type used **to store characters is char**.

2. Character is **16 bits wide in Java**.

3. Java uses **Unicode to represent characters**.

4. Java support lot of Unicode symbols from many more human languages for this purpose, it requires 16 bits.

5. The range of a char is **0 to 65,536**.

6. There are **no negative chars**.

What is Unicode ?

Unicode defines a fully international character set that can represent all of the characters found in all human languages.

Live Example 1 : Integer Value Assigned to Character Data Type

```java
class CharDemo {
  public static void main(String args[]) {
    char ch;

    ch = 'M';
    System.out.println("Character is : " + ch);

  }
}
```

Output :

```
Character is : M
```

Live Example 2 : Integer Value Assigned to Character Data Type

```java
// Demonstrate char data type.
class CharDemo {
  public static void main(String args[]) {
    char ch1, ch2;
```

```java
    ch1 = 88; // code for X
    ch2 = 'Y';

    System.out.print("ch1 and ch2: ");
    System.out.println(ch1 + "" + ch2);
  }
}
```

Output :

```
ch1 and ch2: X Y
```

Live Example 3 : Incrementing Character Variable

```java
class CharDemo2 {
  public static void main(String args[]) {
    char ch1;

    ch1 = 'P';
    System.out.println("ch1 contains " + ch1);

    ch1++; // increment ch1
    System.out.println("ch1 is now " + ch1);
  }
}
```

Output :

```
ch1 contains P
```

```
ch1 is now Q
```

boolean Data Type : Primitive Data Type in Java Programming

1. Boolean is **primitive data type in Java**.

2. Boolean data type is used for **logical values**.

3. Boolean data type can have two possible values : **true or false**.

4. Boolean is the type **returned by all relational operators**

5. Boolean is the type required **by the conditional expressions** used in control statements such as if and for.

6. "Boolean" is wrapper class for "boolean" primitive data type.

How to Declare & Display Boolean Variable ?

[468×60]

```
public static void main(String args[]) {

boolean b1,b2,b3;

b1 = true;   // Assigning Value
b2 = false;  // Assigning Value
b3 = b2;     // Assigning Variable
```

```java
    System.out.println(b1); // Printing Value
    System.out.println(b2); // Printing Value
    System.out.println(b3); // Printing Value


}
```

true

false

false

Live Example :

```java
// Demonstrate boolean values.
class BoolTest {
    public static void main(String args[]) {
```

```
    boolean b1;

    b1 = false;
    System.out.println("b1 is " + b1);
    b1 = true;
    System.out.println("b1 is " + b1);

  // a boolean value can control the if statement
    if(b1) System.out.println("This is executed.");

    b = false;
    if(b)
      System.out.println("Not executed.");

 // outcome of relational operator is a boolean
    System.out.println("100 > 90 is " + (100 > 90));
  }
}
```

Output :

```
b1 is false
b1 is true
This is executed.
100 > 90 is true
```

[468×60]

Different Ways of Using Boolean Value :

Way 1 : Inside If Statement

```java
public static void main(String args[])
{
  boolean b;

  b = true;

  if(b)
    {
    System.out.println("I am True");
    }
}
```

- Boolean Value is used to check whether condition is true or not.

- No need to do == to check equality

```java
public static void main(String args[])
{
  boolean b;

  b = true;

  if(b == true)
    {
    System.out.println("I am True");
    }
}
```

Way 2 : Comparing Two Numbers

```java
class Demo {

public static void main(String args[]) {

  boolean b;

  b = (10 > 6);

  if(b)
    {
    System.out.println("10 > 6");
    }
  }
}
```

we can use boolean value to hold the result Comparison operators. here 10 > 6 therefor true will be stored in boolean variable

In the previous topics we have learnt about the Java variables and their types. We assign the value to the variable, this article will show you how to use the Java integer literal effectively and some of the illegal examples that should be avoided by the programmer.

Java integer literal

Theoretically Literal means – Any number,Text or Other information that represents a **value**.

Different Values that can be assigned to Integer Variable (Integer data type Literal) are –

1. Decimal Literals

2. Octal Literals

3. Hexadecimal Literals

4. Binary Literals

5. Long Literals

6. Values with Underscore in Between

Must Read : Logic to convert the decimal number to hexadecimal number

Literal Types

Literal Type	Assignment Statement	Explanation

Decimal	`int num = 20;`	Decimal 20 is assigned to the variable num
Octal	`int num = 020;`	"**020**" is octal number , so first octal number is converted into integer and then it is assigned to variable "**num**"
Hexadecimal	`int num = 0x20;`	"**0x20**" is hexadecimal number , It is first converted into Decimal then assigned to variable "**num**"
Binary	`int num = 0b1010;`	"**0b1010**" is binary number , assigned to the variable "**num**" after converting it into decimal number
Long	`long num = 563L;`	"**562L**" is long number , assigned to the variable "**num**"

Java integer literal and Underscore

1. In JDK 7, we can embed one or more underscores in an integer literal.

2. It makes easier to read large integer literals.

3. When the literal is compiled, the underscores are discarded.

```
int num = 19_90;
```

4. Java compiler will discard '_' from the above number and **will assign 1990** to variable "num". Thus it is as good as writing –

```
int num = 1990;
```

Literal	Using Underscore	Actual Value
Integer Literal	45_89	4589
Octal Literal	045_23	Equivalent Octal : 04523
Hexadecimal Literal	0x56_23	Equivalent Hex : 0x5623
Binary Literal	0b1000_1001	Equivalent Binary : 10001001

Note : Using Underscore in Integer

1. Don't Use Underscore as first and last character.

2. It is used to read long number easily.

Illegal ways of using underscore

Below are some places where we cannot put the underscore while using the Java integer literal –

1. We cannot put underscore at the beginning or end of a number

2. Underscore should not be placed adjacent to a decimal point in a floating point literal

3. Use of underscore prior to an F or L suffix is illegal

4. Underscore should not be used in positions where a string of digits is expected

Floating Point Literal : Primitive Data Type in Java Programming

1. Decimal values with a fractional component is called floating point.

2. They can be expressed in either **standard or scientific notation**.

[468×60]

Standard Notation

1. Standard notation consists of a whole number component followed by a decimal point followed by a fractional component.

2. For example : 78.0, 3.14159 represent valid **standard-notation floating-point numbers**.

Scientific Notation

1. Scientific notation uses a standard-notation, floating-point number plus a suffix that specifies a power of 10 by which the number is to be multiplied.

2. The exponent is indicated by an E or e followed by a decimal number, **which can be positive or negative**.

3. Valid Examples are :

   o 6.02E21

   o 314159E–05

   o 2e+100.

4. Floating-point literals in Java default to **double precision**.

[468×60]

Literal	Representation	Size	Default
Floating Point Number	F or f	32 bits	–
Double Number	D or d	64 bits	It is default type

Live Example : Assigning Values to Floating Point Literal

```
public static void main(String args[])
{
double d1 = 45.6;
float  f1 = 32.5;
}
```

Short Notes :

1. Jdk 7 also provides us facility for writing hexadecimal literal but they are rarely used.

2. We can use Underscore inside Literals.

```
double num = 1_567_2_82.0;
```

The Scope and Lifetime of Variables :

1. We can declare variables **within any block**.

2. Block is begun with an **opening curly brace and ended by a closing curly brace**.

3. 1 block equal to 1 new scope in Java thus each time you start a new block, you are **creating a new scope**.

4. A scope determines what objects are visible to other parts of your program. It also determines the **lifetime of those objects**.

Live Example 1 : Variable Scope in Java Programming

```java
// Demonstrate block scope.
class Scope {
  public static void main(String args[])
  {
  int n1; // Visible in main

  n1 = 10;

  if(n1 == 10)
   {
   // start new scope
   int n2 = 20; // visible only to this block

   // num1 and num2 both visible here.
   System.out.println("n1 and n2 : "+ n1 +""+ n2);
   }
   // n2 = 100; // Error! y not known here

   // n1 is still visible here.
    System.out.println("n1 is " + n1);
  }
}
```

Output :

```
n1 and n2 : 10 20
n1 is 10
```

1. n1 is declared in main block thus it is **accessible in main block**.

2. n2 is declared in if block thus it is only **accessible inside if block**.

3. Any attempt to access it outside block will **cause compiler time error**.

4. Nested Block can have access to its outermost block. [if block is written inside main block thus all the variables declared inside main block are accessible in if block]

Live Example 2 : How we get Compile Error

```java
class ScopeInvalid {
  public static void main(String args[]) {
    int num = 1;
    {                    // creates a new scope
      int num = 2; // Compile-time error
                   // num already defined
    }
  }
}
```

will cause compile error because variable "num" is declared in main scope and thus it is accessible to all the innermost blocks. However we can try this –

```java
class ScopeInvalid {
```

```java
public static void main(String args[]) {
    {                    // creates a new scope

      int num = 1;

    }

    {                    // creates a new scope

      int num = 2;

    }

  }
}
```

Live Example 3 : Re Initializing Same Variable again and again

```java
class LifeTime {
  public static void main(String args[]) {
    int i;

    for(i = 0; i < 3; i++) {
      int y = -1;
      System.out.println("y is : " + y);
    }
  }
}
```

Output :

```
y is : -1
y is : -1
y is : -1
```

1. Variable "y" is declared inside for loop block.

2. Each time when control goes inside "For loop Block" , Variable is declared and used in loop.

3. When control goes out of the for loop then the variable becomes inaccessible.

This Is A Small Introduction to Learn Java In Few Days
.. I Hope This Book Can Help You

Salem .M Kennedy